The Unseen Rounds: Perspectives from a Patient Care Assistant

Mallika Desai

BookLeaf Publishing

India | USA | UK

Presentation by *BookLeaf Publishing*

Web: www.bookleafpub.com

E-mail: info@bookleafpub.com

ISBN: 9789363314658

First edition 2024

To my family, wonderful mentors who are too numerous to list here, and Ruth, who was the beginning of this journey. This is just the beginning.

ACKNOWLEDGEMENT

Brainstorming and editing assistance was utilized via Chat-GPT for Poems 15-17 and 21. I believe in learning about and safely experimenting with new technology and how it can assist first-time writers like me! No identifying patient information was used, as the poems are fictional and largely based on my emotions to situations working at a hospital, dreams I had after working at the hospital, or imagined situations.

Cover image source: https://pin.it/osn5IOkcn, last accessed May 31, 2024.

Behind the hospitAl Nurse's station desK

Eighteen needs water
  Twenty-two's call light keeps going off
THIRTY TWO's BED ALARM, SOMEONE
GET IT NOW
  Did fifteen not get dinner yet
      Sixteen needs a bath. Please tell me she
cooperated for vitals

In the sterile halls of the buzzing hospital,
We refer to patients as the four walls they're
confined by,
Arguing that we're safeguarding their identity
and privacy
But these numbers melting into the cacophony
of alarms, beeps, curi8us typing, and medical
jargon,
Fast-walk2ng and cart-push2ng
Are the numbers confining their identities
beyond the four-walled box we put them in?
Do they become secrets hidden in a safe in our
minds,
The numbers a passcode, a barrier of entry,
Locking away our prospects of truly making a
connection?

Here are tales of the wonder I found inside the
vault
The words left unsaid, what kept me awake at
night
The juxtaposition of the objective and the
unknown

Sincerely,
A green patient care assistant

Prelude: Am I hurting or helping?

I'm nervous and in awe
Afraid that I'll touch the counter and
contaminate someone's chances of healing
A deep breath, taking in my first official
healthcare role
A step closer to my dream, I think, walking past
the sliding doors
Here are where lives save-

A stocky figure steps into my view
Go print out your patient list,
Who is thi - I'm your preceptor for the day

Thisisthestockroomhere'sthewaterstationthere'se
verythingyou'llneedhere'syourpagerphone
Wedovitalsthreetofourtimesashift
Watchmeandthenyoutry, ohnonotlikethat

You be taking way too long for vitals baby
you're almost at the next round now
I'll time you next time
Why are you taking so long?

As I walk into a patient room for the first time
I feel like a trespasser at dawn
Watching them fast asleep and surrounded by
whirring machines
Wires encircling them like ivy in a deserted
house for one
In the center of a dark room
I doubt why they've been entrusted to me in the
first place
Should I shake them awake… I don't want to
disturb their rest, they're finally resting… but I
need these vitals now… I think I hurt the
previous woman when I shoved the metal
temperature rod in her mouth at the wrong
angle… Twelve grimaced when I put on the
blood pressure cuff on the wrong hand…

I can't help but feel like if I push a little too hard
they'll
Wither into the ashes I'm supposed to help
prevent
I shuffle around the room in a panic wondering
what to do
Watching as their nostrils flare with every inhale
and deflate exhale is strangely peaceful, I muse
They deserve a few more seconds of peace,
being trapped in a hospital

The lights switch on,

Grumbles drift from the patient bed
Echoed by the arrival of my preceptor

Girl you better start speaking up or they aren't
gonna hear you
You aren't going to hurt them by doing your job
but you will hurt them if you don't babe

Today was not what I thought it would be.

I's and O's

Monitoring every single food and fluid that goes
into a patient
Feels a bit like we treat you as a Dr. Seuss
machine
We gatekeep every morsel that goes in
Anticipate what comes out

But I've always wondered what goes on in a
"Star On and Off" machine, Dr. Seuss
What's behind the knobs and twisting pipes
The breathy cough and the twitching eyes

We take I's and O's
Far more than three in a row
But do we really know
The person that lays beneath
The person we behold?

(un)Dressing

Peeling back one curtain after another
Separated by layers of latex and cloth
But also the pitches and shapes of our words
I saw a young woman completely and utterly
alone

Alone with the doubts encircling her like the
tangle of tan blankets in which she lay
How was she going to pay for this luxurious yet
doomsworthy stay

Barr|eras

Beautiful tan, leather skin and dark eyes
Reflecting slight confusion, alight with worry
A furrowed eyebrow and subtle palm-wiping
Four pairs of feet shifting-
 Left
   Right
     Back
       Left

Dry cracked hands, and tired eyes
Ushering hastily, plagued by frustration
A pager ringing and impatient tapping
Broken Spanish laced with helplessness-

"No entrada"
     No mask, no entry
        NO SIR, I CANNOT LET YOU
SEE HER SHE IS CONTACT PRECAUTION

Vocal crescendos don't solve blank stares.

HystERia

"She's shouting again, tell her to use her call
light"
"She shouts as soon as you leave the room, she's
just looking for attention"

As she lays alone, her voice fills the room and
the halls
Masking the emptiness that engulfs her
No one is here, so she pictures her husband's
arms enveloping her
Where is he she asks
No, it can't be- and she wails in agony, reliving
the death of her love
All over again, in every round we make

She fills the air with the last evidence of their
love
The pain she basks in his loss, the scars she is
left
But she is no longer alone

It's not a lack of lucidity nor encephalopathy
It's not her womanly abstrusity
Simply, her melody keeps her company

Code Blue

CALL A CODE BLUE
All of a sudden, we are swept into chaos
Someone's frantically paging any physician they
can find
Supplies get thrown on the floor
We become a wave of chaos and fear

In the center of the room
I see a tinge of blue creep into her skin
Blue like the sky bordering the setting sun
A hue of ocean blue

My feet are planted, like feet stuck in sand
I think of science class where we learned that
We all came from the ocean at some point

In a moment of fear, swept in the tides of
emotions
I wonder if this is nature's way of returning her
to where we all came from

Mirror

Bending down to pick up a blood pressure cuff
I startle, seeing the neat pleats of a saree
greeting me
My first Indian patient! I think excitedly

The elderly woman asks me if I have refrigerator
to store her daal
So I refrigerate it, half tempted to eat it myself,
missing my own mom's food

I don't get her at all! My coworker sighs with
exasperation later
This woman keeps asking for something new
every five minutes

I could see my own mom doing that
Hovering over me and coming in with a list of
concerns
She would sneak some khichdi and kheer if I
asked for it
Apple sauce and some gatorade, fretting about
me not being fed enough
She would ask the nurses all the side effects of
each medication

And sit in the corner with me, reading her
prayers from her phone

For some reason, my skin color being the same
as hers
The food habits shared
They all meant something

I could understand and smile, while my
colleague didn't
And when I had a patient who didn't share that,
it was harder for me to relate as well

Our backgrounds are a unique strength and a
weakness
The smile and understanding should be for
everyone
Regardless if they wear a sari, a hijab, or Levi's

Midas

King Midas famously requested the Greek god
Dionysus
That everything he touch become gold
But once responsibility became reality and
realized
He wanted to get rid of it
So Dionysus let him put his hands in the river
And the river paid the consequences
Hardening along its river bed

On my first day, I was warned of a Midas
A Midas was something you got when you did
something wrong
Something you got when you endangered a
patient or the hospital
As I understood it, but I never really understood
it at first

Why would we be punished for switching the
leads on an electrocardiogram
We could just do it again and print another on

As patient care assistants, we seek the honor and
golden responsibility of caring for patients

Often before we're far along in our overall
careers and wise enough to understand the
responsibility
But it is nothing like we expect, both with its
immense joys and sorrows

When we misplace leads, we put the patient at
risk of an incorrect diagnosis
We endanger lives and doctor's decisions

The gold does have a shadow
But one that we can light with our thoroughness
and care

The Nurse's Station

Our days start early, often before the sun rises
The nurse's station starts out as the home of
bleary eyed, overworked nurses
Getting ready to go home, be with their families,
finally eat some dinner
As well as the next shift's nurses
Catching up on the night's event concerning
patients and colleagues they don't always see
Carrying funny videos of their toddler or new
snack recommendations at Kroger
The smell of coffee and the clanking of Stanley
tumblers intermingles with the sounds of the
printer's staccato as it spits out the list of
patients for the shift
The nurse's station is abuzz at shift change

Throughout the shift, the station is a hive of our
colony
The worker bees, the PCAs like me and new
nurses,
and the queens - the charge nurse and the HUC,
Gather at the hub
With occasional visits from rounding physicians
and family members in need of directions

We go out into the halls and rooms, do our jobs,
Instead of pollinating, we take vitals and deliver
meals
And then we return to our queens, reporting the
day's events
What patients we helped, instead of flowers

The cycle repeats, new bees coming in and
others going out
The nurse's station is anything but stationary

Popping the Pepsi Bubble

I was rarely allowed to drink soda as a kid
For good reason, we were taught it was sugary
That advertising was just a business scheme
You couldn't be that happy drinking soda

So I always wondered why soda was served with
almost every hospital meal
Wasn't the hospital supposed to be bringing
patients back to health?

Through training, I found that this was because
they were clear liquids
And could help elevate low blood sugar after
fasting for surgery

But I just couldn't shake the feeling every time I
served a soda
That I was somehow harming the patient, with
my parent's voices echoing in my head

With a heavy heart, I brought a Pepsi can into a
patient's room
And was met with a chuckle

Did you know that I worked for Pepsi?

Ah, I could always tell the difference between
Pepsi and any other soda

His eyes eyes sparkled, as he beamed at me,
telling me stories of how he found his job,
narrating memories of making his family try to
guess the difference between different sodas

Perhaps soda could bring joy, not in the way I
thought
Reality superimposed on assumptions will
always surprise you,
Challenge you
And it's the best part of this job

Skin

Every specialty, hospital, and position has
different rules about scrubs
Some places require hospital colored scrubs
But a different hue for operating rooms
They are practically our skin, as we wear the
same ones each day

Pediatric nurses wear fun ones with bright,
playful colors
And surgeons don ciel blue
Other attendings wear business casual, coated in
white

White coats are symbols of trust and
professionalism
But sometimes a beacon of elitism or simply a
germ transmitting device

Our clothes are up to interpretation, our actions
are up to interpretation
Our backgrounds and skin color are up to
interpretation
Uniforms are meant to promote teamwork and
unity
But will they ever?

The Infiltrated Army

An army of doctors crowds around the doorway
What's happening, I ask the charge nurse
A liver transplant, responds

Alcoholism impacts one's liver
As the liver is the soldier that breaks down the
alcohol consumed
When the soldier becomes too wounded, the
only solution is replacing the soldier itself

And therefore a liver transplant is necessary
But in most transplants, a foreign organ is
infiltrating the army,
And the army is trained to attack foreign bodies
So immunosuppressant medications must be
used

Suppressants must be used to amplify growth
and recuperation
Watching the crowd of professionals putting
their brilliant minds together to pull the patient
through a miracle
I pray that the patient's journey till this point
will foster growth and recuperation
A redirection onto a healthier path
Honoring the sacrifice that someone kind and
brave gave for a stranger to have a new life

Just Keep Pushing

The nurse's cart is a computer on wheels
Sounds like it would make rounds easier right?
Instead it veers off randomly, the wheels seem to
go anywhere but straight

A shift is much like the cart
One minute, you are exactly on track - on
schedule, one could venture to say (cautiously)
And another minute, the sitter has disappeared,
two bed alarms are going off
You can't get ahold of the nurse and your phone
keeps going off

A patient care assistant's job is to make the lives
of patients and nurses easier
But sometimes, you're in the eye of the tornado
and only seem to be tearing down the wrong
houses instead of just destroying a grassy field

The nurse's cart is a computer on wheels
Sounds like it would make rounds easier right?
Instead it veers off randomly, the wheels seem to
go anywhere but straight

A shift is much like the cart

One minute, you are exactly on track - on
schedule, one could venture to say (cautiously)
And another minute, the sitter has disappeared,
two bed alarms are going off
You can't get ahold of the nurse and your phone
keeps going off

A patient care assistant's job is to make the lives
of patients and nurses easier
But sometimes, you're in the eye of the tornado
and only seem to be tearing down houses instead
of just destroying a grassy field

But at the end of the day, the cart and you find
your calm
You catch the phone that is thrown at you, and
you figure out exactly what your patient needs
You have a quick laugh with a patient's family
member
And most importantly, you help a patient feel
even 1% better

That's why you keep pushing the cart

Finding a Home

"Be careful, the patient has lice
They've been homeless and high for weeks now,
I heard"

Healthcare professionals are taught to be caring
in every scenario
Some situations still make them uncomfortable
However, the difference is that our duty is to
choose kindness every time

I entered the room to find him curled up in the
center of the bed
In the sterile light of the clinic's room,
Their presence cut through the silent gloom.
With matted hair and a distant gaze,
Their life etched out in a foggy haze.

"Please," they whispered, voice barely there,
As I donned my gloves with utmost care.
Lice crawled freely through tangled strands,
A plight untended by gentle hands.

Their skin, like parchment, dry and thin,
A map of sorrow marked within.
Each tiny creature a visible woe,

In the tangled nest where hardships grow.

I brushed and combed with tender grace,
Washing away the disgrace,
For in these moments, pure and clear,
I saw beyond their outer veneer.

We spoke of dreams long cast aside,
Of places loved and people who'd died.
In their tales, both sad and profound,
I found a humanity that knows no bound.

A patient care assistant, that's my role,
But in this moment, I mend more than the
whole.
For every stroke of the comb in my hand,
Is a promise that someone understands.

The clinic's hum, a backdrop to care,
In this haven, there's room to share.
To see beyond the grime and the plight,
And offer solace in the dead of night.

When dawn breaks and they walk away,
I hope they carry some hope to stay.
For in their eyes, a flicker of grace,
A spark rekindled in this sacred space.

And though the road ahead is tough,

The kindness shared is just enough.
To remind them they are not alone,
In this world, compassion can atone.

Personal Protective Equipment

In the dawn's soft glow, I start my day,
Donning armor in a silent ballet.
A mask, a shield, gloves pulled tight,
In this war, I stand upright.

Polyester and latex, a second skin,
To shield the world from the germs within.
A barrier against the unseen foe,
In these halls where life ebbs and flows.

Gowns like cloaks, boots on feet,
Creating a fortress in this sterile suite.
Each piece a promise, each layer a vow,
To guard and protect, here and now.

Through the fabric, I feel the beat,
Of hearts in rhythm, fast and fleet.
Eyes peeking over the surgical mask,
A patient's plea, a silent ask.

Behind this shield, I see your pain,
A mirrored reflection, the human strain.
Though plastic and cloth keep us apart,
My hands reach out with an open heart.

In muffled whispers, care transcends,
Through barriers, a connection extends.
For in each touch, though gloved and sealed,
A deeper compassion is revealed.

This armor worn, a daily rite,
In this battle, day and night.
Yet in my heart, beneath the gear,
Lives the pledge to always be near.

When the day is done, the gown comes off,
The mask, the shield, the latex cloth.
I breathe in deeply, unburdened, free,
But the duty remains, eternally.

In every glove, in every mask,
Lies the essence of our task.
To heal, to comfort, to always care,
Even through the barriers we wear.

For in this garb, though we are bound,
It's our humanity that is truly profound.
No wall of fabric can divide,
The empathetic heart we carry inside.

The Eleventh Hour

Weary hands still offering care,
Night whispers of dawn.

Masks and gloves intact,
Compassion's touch unspoken,
Hope threads through the dark.

Silent halls echo,
Patient hearts beat steady, strong,
Daylight soon to break.

In this quiet hour,
Strength and solace intertwined,
We stare at the clock, willing it to move faster.

An Older Colleague

Kind around the edges,
She would not take no for an answer, nothing
less than perfect.
At times stern like a mother,
And at others, packaging and saving a little food
for families who needed it most
Even against the rules.

What Goes Around Doesn't Always Come Around

There have been many times where I wonder
why someone is facing the perils they are
Their goodness shines through even in pain and
amidst worry
Is there really divine justice if they are the ones
who suffer

One of my patients was an ambulance driver
A faithful one who drove into crises to rescue
others
I imagine his calm reassurance as he helps a
patient into the back of his vehicle
Weaving through traffic and being a loyal
teammate, working alongside paramedics

And now he is bedridden, restless,
He must have his table a certain way, his plates a
certain angle
Maybe he feels helpless enough to want to retain
his control over what remains

The best I can do is be there,
Be attentive,
Be the same steady he was for others

The Good Doctor

Physicians are often regarded as otherworldly
role models,
Saviors, possessors of almost all answers
Dr. William J. Mayo, a pioneer said
"Individually, no man is respected more highly
than the physician."

Sitting in the nurses station, disputes can
sometimes beg to differ
It is natural for conflict to be present
Especially in high stress environments
permeated by hierarchy
Which helps bring efficient care to patients
But often inspires further friction rather than
forgiveness

Some physicians acknowledge us as PCAs, the
bottom of the food chain,
And other others don't, drowning in a
never-ending list of tasks
Some help us turn a patient when they see us
struggling or even get a patient water
Even though it isn't their job
While others catch a quick breather so they can
make the right decision for a patient

In their hands, they hold the ability to change
someone's life
Even in an instant or a decade down the line

Nurses are the true caregiver of a patient
Giving medications, changing bandaging,
Contacting family members, paging physicians
Directing patient-care assistant

But no matter how much responsibility one has,
I have observed thus far that both professionals
are far happier
When there is mutual respect and
communication of intention

To someone, scrolling on a phone in an
approved location could look like slacking or
being behind on notes,
But perhaps a physician or nurse needed that
brief break
To be in the right frame of mind to be present for
patients and the whole team.

Back and Forth

In lectures, thoughts begin to stray,
To patients fighting through their day.
Every smile, each carefree jest,
Feels weightless, easy, unlike the rest.

While classmates stress on seemingly mundane
worries,
I recall faces, hidden throes.
In this bubble, problems seem small,
Compared to those who've seen it all.

Back and forth, I tread two lands,
One of leisure, one of hands.
Mending wounds and soothing fears,
Echoes of pain lace my thoughts.

College life, a contrast clear,
Problems vanish, nothing severe.
Yet in my heart, the weight remains,
Of hospital nights and silent pains.

Between the books and midnight shifts,
My perspective constantly drifts.
Seeing life through dual lenses,
One of ease, one of defenses.